POEMS *seeking* READERS

Poems, new to the area, seek readers looking for love, for intimacy, or for each other.

"Nutrition Facts" seeks health-conscious reader to share Bran Flakes.

"Anticipation" seeks a girl starving her body into a hanger.

"C Major" seeks reader who took piano lessons. Basic music theory a plus.

"Dip" seeks friend to eat leftovers with.

"Hero" seeks reader who enjoys watching movies where men fight in slow motion.

"Echolalia" wants a reader who gets what he/she wants.

"Idioglossia" seeks lost twin to concoct secret language and hunt rabbits.

"Condition" seeks reader to program in classic behaviourist fashion. How you doin?

"American History" seeks literate — though not necessarily literal — fish.

"Again" seeks reader to swallow eyes, beer caps, or batteries.

"Hangman" seeks stickman intent on saving its life.

"Stranger" seeks reader tired of pretending to understand poems.

PERSONALS

FREEHAND BOOKS

WOMEN SEEKING MEN

Classy, soph, business owner, progressive, seeks SM 45+ lib-wit, witty, for wine and can-...

...d and depressed) seeking chal-...

A cute & near retirement. Plan for sweet M 55-75. Back-ambulatory 75+ filthy rich.

SF, 22, seeks SM w... black suit for one time...

...adve... sionate... lationship... Abs no facial...

PERSONALS

Poems by Ian Williams

Parents visiting. Already in I... rel. Seeks SM. Fluent Tamil a... Hindi a must. Generous c...

Recent widow seeks... 70+ for remainder...

© Ian Williams 2012

 Canada Council **Conseil des Arts**
for the Arts **du Canada**

Freehand Books gratefully acknowledges the support of the Canada Council for the Arts for its publishing program. ¶ Freehand Books, an imprint of Broadview Press Inc., acknowledges the financial support for its publishing program provided by the Government of Canada through the Canada Book Fund.

Freehand Books
515 – 815 1st Street SW Calgary, Alberta T2P 1N3
www.freehand-books.com

Book orders: LitDistCo
100 Armstrong Avenue Georgetown, Ontario L7G 5S4
Telephone: 1-800-591-6250 Fax: 1-800-591-6251
orders@litdistco.ca www.litdistco.ca

LIBRARY AND ARCHIVES CANADA CATALOGUING IN PUBLICATION
Williams, Ian, 1979–
Personals / Ian Williams.

Poems.
ISBN 978-1-55481-104-5

I. Title.

PS8645.I4448P47 2012   C811'.6   C2012-900307-7

Edited by Robyn Read and Owen Percy
Book design by Natalie Olsen, www.kisscutdesign.com
Author photo by Dustin Marshall

Printed on FSC recycled paper and bound in Canada

FOR MY

CONTENTS

Define loneliness?

Yes.

It's what we can't do for each other.

CLAUDIA RANKINE

Don't Let Me Be Lonely

I

Problem is our armpits and crotches are feathered
with cobwebs. Problem is she leaks soft-boiled eggs
or I package seedless grapes. Problem is her parents
made us wait until they had crossed the width
of my nose. Problem is she had a migraine. Problem is
we did not want children. Problem is we did
not want each other until too late. Problem is I can't be
late for work in the morning. Problem is this morning
she says she dreamt she was holding a sandwich bag
of crickets. Problem is I am already late and listening
to the weather. Problem is we don't speak
to the problem. Problem is the school bus
that stops in front of our townhouse just as I'm reversing

the problem is we don't know

I would have taken the child sitting in a shopping cart,
the one her eye swaddled. I would have killed every child
under two, except the one floating on the Nile and the one
on donkeyback to Egypt. I would have still married her. I would
have picked through every dumpster, gently, to avoid wounding
the soft skull. I would have followed a teenager into a restroom
and reached my hands under the stall. I would have saved
myself in ice cube trays in the deep freezer. I would have braved
the security cameras in the neonatal ward and snuck out
a bundle under my coat. I would have demanded
a child for stealing my radishes. I would have spun straw
to gold. I would have built a little boy out of wood
and presented him to my wife along with a talking cricket. I
would have delivered if I knew for sure she would

I should have lasted longer. I should have left earlier
because the roads are slick with albumen. I should not have
cancelled the appointment with the white coat. I should have
worn boxers. I should have sold my mountain bike
when I turned forty. I should not have played StarCraft
on my laptop on my lap. I should have played
Barry White instead. I should have worn cologne
and set the table with candles. I should have chirped
sweetly and mussed her hair when she told me
she dreamt crickets. I should have hopped on her. I should
have thought about children when her father warned
her to think about the children. I should have found her
a sultan. I should have left earlier. I should have lasted longer but

what a man has to work with.

Like, a girl on our lawn says, you want to hear me talk
like my sister when she's on the phone? Like she always
says *like*. Like this. Like me and my boyfriend
went to the mall and like I saw him looking at a girl
and like she was totawy into him. Like I can tell.
Like she was all, you know, like fwirting with him
like I wasn't there but like then I looked at her and she
like gave me a look like I can look at him if I want
to look at him, like they're my eyes. Like I got so mad
I like wanted to totawy kiw her.

                                     Like, my wife tells me
from her pillow in the dark, I am a pop can
with the tab broken and rattling around inside.
Like I might as well be a man. Like what is the point of *being a woman if you can't make another her*

So, a boy on our lawn says, I digged a hole
and put some water in it so my Transformer
could grow into a giant Transformer airplane gun
so when I shoot my laser *piu piu* I can fly away
up to the sun so you'll never catch me, so you'll never
shoot me, so you'll never ever ever ever ever ever
get me.
                              So, my wife tells me
from her pillow in the dark, some of the crickets
in the sandwich bag were brittle — crickets are known
to eat their dead, you know — so I couldn't
be sure if I was eating dead or live crickets so I just
ate whatever my hand found so I must have eaten
some live ones so inside me sounded like night so as

you can see we will never have a baby

Then our child gets croup and turns us into raccoons.
Then our child gets better. Then our child starts chanting
in Latin and sneezing in Greek. Then our child walks
en pointe. Then our child has a crisis because it wants
to be a Komodo dragon in the school play but
only gets to be a lizard. Then our child falls asleep
in a chocolate factory. Then our child wakes up
in its teens. Then our child gets braces and glasses
and begins to glitter. Then our child smokes in the mirror.
Then our child leaves us. Then our child leaves us alone.
Then our child calls on Sunday. Then our child
meets someone else's child and has its own child.
Then our child stands over our beds brushing back the nurses. Then

what happens to us what happens to our child is what happens to us what

Of course we did not turn into raccoons or crickets.
Of course we sleep well and wake well and on Sundays
do the jumble. Of course I regret not going to Venice
for our honeymoon. Of course the Falls are not the same.
Of course I never say the word *barren*
even when she looks like she is wearing the desert.
Of course she never says *sterile* when I come
out of the shower, buffing small circles into my
stainless steel chest. Of course we have priced
African babies. Of course we can't drive by
a Chinese restaurant without craving a little
girl. Of course our DNA is in a sealed envelope
in a locked drawer in a locked cabinet in a locked house

of course our child would look like us

But we did not want children. But we did
not want a townhouse either. But we got
a townhouse in a field of children with round
dimpled faces. But we did not want girls.
But we saw them in ribbon and crinoline
at church. But we did not want boys. But
we saw them squeezing frogs near the ravine.
But we did not want children. But they knocked
on our door with UNICEF cartons and chocolate
almonds. But we did not buy. But we bought.
But they wore soccer uniforms and ballet leotards
under their winter coats. But they sat in their mother's
car as she dropped off the Avon. But we were surrounded by pregnant women who grew round around

Or we could get a Pekingese. *Give me children, or else I die.*
Or a Siamese cat. *Give me children, or else I die.* Or we could
redecorate with glass and steel and pointy corners
in the best modern way. *Give me children, or else I die.* Or else
move to a ch-ching penthouse. *Give me children,*
or else I die. Or throw parties and serve canapés. *Give me*
children, or else I die. Or travel by train from farther to further
every spring. *Give me children, or else I die.* Or we could spend
the evenings counting our gold. *Give me children, or else*
I die. Or become the cool aunt and uncle. *Give me children,*
or else I die. Or sponsor a child or buy a goat. *Give me children,*
or else I die. Or buy a hybrid or recycle more or run
a shelter or feed the poor or bike for cancer or knit for preemies

give me children or else give me children or else give me children or else

And I find her by the sink rinsing broccoli
in a colander. And outside the roads are covered
in sperm. And she tells me about the children
littering the lawn. And she tells me one of them left
an empty chip bag and another an empty
juice box under our tree. And spores of broccoli
swim through the holes, waving their tails. And I can't
reverse in the morning, I say, I can't reverse.
And she nearly went out there in her housecoat
and slippers with a broom. And why can't she
have one, just one, to fatten or else to put in the oven?
And sometimes when I leave and she hears the garage
rumble shut, she worries I will hit the road and never come back

no more no more no more no more no more no

Name. Permanent address. Mailing address (if different).
Will you want me when I ask you to vacuum the stairs
with the hose attachment? Daytime telephone number.
when we are eating cabbage for the third straight night?
Evening. Cell. Email. when you hear my footsteps
descend the basement stairs during the Leafs game?

Date of birth. Sex. Marital status. Will you want me
when birds walk across my face? Employment
in the last two years. and I give up mowing
my legs? From. To. give up dusting my cheeks?
From. To. give up Restylane?

                                            Emergency
contact information. when I sit on the toilet seat
of the ensuite weeping? Name. over a clot of blood?
Relationship. over nothing? Telephone. Would you if I migrate
my mind into a key of winter afternoons from the Depression?
Type of card. Name on card. Card number. if I start calling
you Mr. Shopkeeper? Date of expiry. if I keep asking you if
you'll be getting any milk soon for the baby?

(Optional) Choose a security question. Would you want me
if I lose a limb? Mother's maiden name. if I lose a breast?
Year of father's birth. Will you want me when
I declare the above statements are true. I lose half of me?
Signature. Date. and half of you?

NUTRITION FACTS

One of us cuts a banana into cereal
with the edge of a spoon and the other reads the side
of the Bran Flakes box.

Might not look like love — Might not love look like
this? No boy plunging headlong from the sky,
no star-shaped marshmallow.

But a kiss on the forehead,
the string of a banana still on the lip, goodbye.

II

He was a young inner city needle who played
ball in a cage : what the needle were we thinking :
I would needle my hands in the chain-link needle
and needle him : he played with his needle
and his abs were needled like a half-eaten
Hershey needle :

                                        I had a
needle when I was seventeen : I told my needle I was
needle and he paid : we had needled each other : of course
it's needlable whether our needle was really a needle
when we decided to needle it : if it was a needle
I would name it Needle : we weren't allowed to needle
after the needle so we never talked about the needle :
my needle dropped out of needle and needled
a six-week certification needle : I needle saw him much :
needle once or twice he came back and brought me needles
for lunch and we needled our needles in the caf in silence
with our chopsticks : I needle you, he said :
I needle you too.

You. At the Tire and Lube Express. You said *lube*
and I — did you notice? — revved. Your name tag
was missing so I read your hair, curled like a string of e's,
your forearms drizzled with soft hairs like a boy's
first moustache. Apart from that, you were built
like a walrus. The kind of man that drives a Ford
pickup. Black or silver. You said, *There might be a gas leak*
and *We can't fix that here, but don't worry, we'll get you fixed.*
By *fixed* you meant *hooked up,* by *hooked up* you meant
in touch with and meant nothing beyond *touch.*

Me. Volvo. Smelled like gasoline: I overfilled the tank
before the oil change. I took the package that comes
with a filter replacement. Have you already forgotten me?
I had trouble with the debit machine. Remember? You said,
Turn your card the other way — remember? — and took my hand,
not the card, took my hand with the card in it
and swiped it through. Remember. Please.
The gasoline. The woman almost on fire.

because it takes three hours and gives him the blues bad
so not now, not now, later, he promises, then falls asleep
on my couch, shrugging his upper lip like a horse.
Open parenthesis. She wore black dresses. They drank a lot
of Beaujolais. She had been to Europe several times.
Spoke another language, French most likely. Worked
for a firm. Had a way of playing with her earlobes
when searching for words. They did not touch. He held
open doors. She had a son. Divorced, divorcing the father.
The father was still involved. *So you understand,* she said.
Right right right, he said. They talked about their money.
They talked about Gare Saint-Lazare. They talked about her
son's teacher. They talked about maybe. There was a moment
in his car when nothing happened. A moment when he thought.
Nothing happened. She leaned toward his lips. *Rien.*
She pulled her earlobe. Closed parenthesis. He doesn't know
where he is or what time it is when he wakes up and he has a long
drive and a trustees' meeting in the morning so not now,
not now, next time, he promises, and gets his harmonica and goes.

Let's say, hypothetically, that he met a separated woman
in the enclosure between the fire doors and the main doors
while waiting for rain to pass. That the way she wore her hood,
low over her eyebrows, made her look Gregorian. And that
he chanted small talk from the oldest manuscript he knew
and asked her if she wanted to have a latte slash cappuccino slash
caramel macchiato to which she said *Te Deum laudamus.*
And since this is hypothetical I could say that they met
in a checkout line and slash or shoulder of an unlit highway
but that wouldn't be right, even hypothetically. So let's stay
with the coffee stand, the rain. Let's say he told her his number
and she dialled right away and that when his phone started beating
he realized that he had not noticed his heart beat his heartbeat
in years. It's as if, he tells me later, it had been set to *Silence All.*
Figuratively, of course. Hypothetically, even, is it safe to assume
that since that afternoon in the church there has been no Latin
between them? that it wasn't raining after all? that he mistakenly
read her hood and her antiphonal mouth as scripture?

I have folded his story into origami and he can't straighten
it out again I have folded their faces and hands in poker
and he can't tell anymore, he can't tell. Question.
If all bacteria unionized and ganged up and spared no soul
save this woman, her ex-husband, and you, who would she choose
to sire Cain and Abel? I can't be sure, he says. Question. Do you think
you might be wasting your time then? I think I might, he says.
Question. What happens to the man she does not choose? He goes
extinct, he says. Question. What if a meteorite hooked you
unconscious, how long would she kneel and blow air into you? Maybe
an hour, he says. An hour's a long time, he says. Question. How long
would you inflate her? Years, he says. Her whole life, he says.
He folds his arms into an airplane. Question. Can you do anything —
Nothing I can do, he says — let me finish, to make her choose you?
He says nothing. He unfolds his wings and flies away.

He does not know if sheep are grazing on his hair at night
or if a peasant woman is shucking his scalp of husk and silk.
He picks a hair from his tongue. He does not know if he is living
beside himself or why the bleating from the apartment next door
never seems to stop. Does the Samaritan sleep with the TV on
because he cannot sleep or because he needs to sleep
with someone? Or if a young pyro crawls into his barn at night
and singes his thinning hay with a lighter. Thou art lost
and gone forever. Dreadful sorry. The cattle are lowing,
O my darling, O my darling, O my darling, Clementine.
What's her name? I ask. I can't tell you that. What can you tell me?
I met someone. The only thing he knows to be as sure as death
is that he must water his vertex twice a day for the rest of his life
or griffins will eat what the sheep have left. He will die
of minoxidil. He brushes hair from his shoulder. And? I say.
You met a woman and? And I met a woman. Period.

I yawned all the while we stood on the prow of a ship
with our arms open in front of a green screen,
I mean, a sunset. The week before I had to watch myself,
my black and white self in a fedora, quick step through lines,
We'll always have Paris, though we were in Morocco, though
we were on a couch, technically, with all her friends
when I charged in and said, *You complete me.* I zoned out
in Stratford in a tomb when I found her dead,
just kidding, she was drugged up. Then when I woke up
at the edge of a lake, her friends were back, this time
as swans, and I wasn't clear on what I was doing
in tights and a mullet. I zoned out again. We went out back
to the dumpster and ate spaghetti — you low down
you dog you sweet thing you — till we kissed, till we boogied.

makes her wonder
where her man is, where all the men are,
whether men exist, whether men be figments
of print only, whether the one real man left
is squatting, a fluorescent frog in the Amazon,
or hibernating cryogenically, body encased
in a glass cylinder of green fluid, whether the bodies
she sees crossing the street are cross-dressed women.

She searched and found but never met a man
on the Internet. The mailbox on his bachelor apartment
said *mr_right* or *truluv1* or some nonsense. If he is real
he has a smooth pelvis and sleeps in a plastic box.
He can be made to walk. He can be made to drive
Barbie's pink car. He cannot be made to order
or to love.

When she was a girl, her father made her
stray a dog. She led it into the backwoods then turned
and jitterbugged home. But the dog would not be left
alone. It would trot behind her, each time
trot behind her, at a distance, trot behind her
and sniff at the door. Were dogs men.

ANTICIPATION

is not the same as waiting.
Horses the size of ants gallop through the veins
beating dust toward the heart. Men in chainmail
storm down axons and fire their crossbows.
A pterodactyl caws. A shark's fin cuts
through gastric acid.

She is playing Solitaire in computer light.
She is starving her body into a hanger.
She is cleaning the bathtub of her hair.
She is talking to digits until her battery dies.
She is counting the months till June on her fingers.
She is counting her fingernails as they dry.

SIXTEEN

Email is fine and a text here and there, your body passing
through light rain and light hits, but I want you to call me.

I float through a bowl of cereal during commercials
late at night. Now might be a good time to call me. *Call me*

on the line. Call me, call me, any anytime. From the sixteenth
century. Cup your hand around your mouth and call me

from 'neath the balcony. In the morning, I find my phone
unlit, but it might be dead. You might have called me —

it. Someday, says the romantic, you'll spot me in Union station
through a crowd of petals on a wet, black bough and call me

Ishmael. *Just call out my name. I love it when you call me Big Papa.*
Cradle your damn pinky and thumb to your face and call me.

The time she called from the esophagus of a bus, giggling
to make it seem like she was talking to her man, sounded G^7.

The time she maxed out her cards and needed a loan
until her tax return — *I promise, I promise* — echoed G^7.

The time she made us prowl Montreal for free wireless
so I could read her cute co-worker's email echoed G^7.

All the times she held sweaters against my chest to see
if they would fit some bastard's marble torso echoed G^7.

The time she needed my arm and shoulder near the produce
because she was being sawed in half echoed G^7.

The time she made me drive to a flammable suburb to meet
her new man and his faux hawk echoed G^7.

The time she drunkenly sang, *Doe, a deer, a female deer,*
at my sister's shower, she never got past the G^7.

should not be
played until the player has played it for two years
or until she has spent two years kissing boys
against the side wall of her parents' garage
after the motion sensor nods off. Whichever
comes later.

I've been told that
the endangered instrument can only be played
with the eyes closed, with a certain moistness
of palm, not too much, that an endangered
female should stand on her toes, an endangered
male tilt his head down. Its call is actually made
at the back of the throat, not the tongue, and no one
can hear it except certain birds and long-necked
mammals that fall asleep in the heat and tangle
of tenderness.

| 9 | 8 | 7 | 6 | 5 | 4 | 3 | 2 | 1 |

The rain has rainbowed
the oil. Go home.

| | 8 | 7 | 6 | 5 | 4 | 3 | 2 | 1 |

A whole floor of bedrooms
and her children gone.

| | | 7 | 6 | 5 | 4 | 3 | 2 | 1 |

car – car – car – car –
car – car – car = yours

| | | | 6 | 5 | 4 | 3 | 2 | 1 |

A full lot wants to be emptied.
An empty lot wants a lot.

| | | | | 5 | 4 | 3 | 2 | 1 |

No trapped neon bee.
No *No Vacancy*.

| | | | | |4|3|2|1|

Could be a lake. Could be a mind.
Place inverts to space. Space to time.

| | | | | | |3|2|1|

Too many teeth smiling
the smile of a skull.

| | | | | | | |2|1|

Between this space and that,
a queen bed, a double plot.

| | | | | | | | |1|

An empty seat at dinner
for two.

| | | | | | | | | |

What was here before all this
nothing? Nothing.

Excel

In the nineteenth century, this office building
used to be a girls' dormitory: a spreadsheet

of xx chromosomes. A now dead girl is sleeping
on the desk, tickled as a man double-clicks her neck.

Word

The now dead girl should have run a spell-check
before she got married, should've hit F7. Hit CTRL Z.

Undo, undo. He's a typo. How come every other
dead girl can see DonJuan underlined in red?

Outlook

But no, she decides to hit send, and DonJuan spams her
every night, forwarding his DNA until the now dead girl's

inbox is jammed with kids. Tiny red flags everywhere.

PowerPoint

The next forty years, her life is read to her, slide by slide
by a balding man in a dark, chilly room. If she wants,

the now dead girl can follow her life on a handout,
a slide for each year, take notes on four blank lines.

Occasionally there's an animation where letters arrive
one by one from other now dead girls on the west coast

Picture Manager

with photos of cliffs and the Pacific and, once, a starlet.
All children are cropped out, brightness adjusted. Contrast

the now dead girl's frames: her soon to be dead children
are powdered in sepia from afar, but up close each one

is made up of the images of all the others,
every pixel a face of its own.

SharePoint, formerly FrontPage

She considers divorcing DonJuan, CTRL F-ing her surname,
replacing all her given to Britney, Brittany, Britnee, Britni.

But what good would that do? Uploading her old self
to her newfangled blog. Local to remote: no one to no one.

Your husband smells
like Irish Spring and soon he will smell like Old Spice.
Mine does too. He has not forgiven you
the pounds of children still belted to your body,
the first boy's lisp, the middle boy's silence, the girl's XX.
Your sons are deaf unless you learn to speak in MP3.
Your daughter studies your body as if it were a new
outbreak. She quarantines your glances and sighs
for her therapist, years after the apocalypse. Your husband
will smell like Old Spice and then like Bengay
and then he will smell like his coffin.

If you need to be touched because no one is touching you
I will touch you, my sweet BBW — the bigger, the better.
The best massage you will get, the deepest rest
this side of death.

Looking for someone
to chill with, drink a few beers, watch some U F C,
maybe some SmackDown too. N O T looking for any action
no potheads no druggies no thugs no wannabes nobody
looking to crash. Prefer non-smoker or smoke outside
or whatever. I'm watching the kids till my wife gets home
from her night class at 10 and my little girl's allergic,
that's why.

Fight's on in a few. Just looking for a regular guy.
But mind the strictly. Never had a dude do nothing to me.
Okay, just once a buddy and I got high back in high
school. His mother was passed out and like I said we were stoned,
stoned and wasted and bored and he tried to put his tongue
in my mouth. Prick.

Hit me up if you want to chill with me,
knock back some brewskies, watch some U F C.

The friends I friended do not show.
One by one, yellow leaves, they text
— the snow, the snow, the snow, the snow —
sad emoticons of their faces.

One by one, down an arpeggio, they text
See you Monday. I will face them and
as always ☺ and ☺ and ☺ my face.
I'll say, Forget about it. I understand.

On Monday I will have to face them and
the snow, the snow, the snow, the snow.
I'll say, Forget it. Really. I understand
the friends I friended did not show.

The hero wins
because that's what heroes do when you spend
the money to buy the DVD of a movie you already
know the ending to, not because you've seen it before
but because you heard from a colleague in HR
that it would make you feel real good after,
it was the best thing she's seen lately, and that's
with her being married and every morning pushing spoons
into the faces of her two children
                              so you watch it
knowing the only thing that will make you feel good
this evening is seeing a bare-chested man wail on another
in a ring and another in a street and another in a ring
in slow-mo and the *dff dff* sounds of the gloves striking
bodies in movies, which don't sound like bodies for real,
not that you'd admit to knowing that,
                              and the hero
doesn't even look like heroes in the real world
which are not the heroes in grade four essays either
but like (stay with me) this one time you dropped by a woman's place
and you were sitting at her kitchen table and she asked you
if you wanted anything to drink and she opened the fridge
and you saw through the crack between her body
and the door only a pitcher of water on the wire shelf
in the yellow light —
                   you want to call her a hero
because she's surviving with her mouth shut
or yourself because you're so affected must mean
you're noble. Go ahead. But there are other words
for you two.

My ex is back with her ex
so I'm looking for someone new. I'm looking for someone else,
for someone up for adult fun, which in my book is straight
forward: nothing kinky, no keys in bowls, no leather, no role
play games with safewords. No emotional mumbojumbo
either. You are not my "girlfriend" but you don't have to be
a slut.

Check me out in the pic below (ask if you want
a headshot). Doesn't really matter what you look like. Really.
Just be real. I'm looking for someone who is not a spambot,
for someone who is not a price, for someone who is not a virus,
for someone who is not my ex, for someone who is not silicone,
for someone who is not the type to hook up with random men
but who found herself here, reading, still reading.

Once one gets what one wants
one no longer wants it.

One no longer wants what?

One no longer wants what
one wanted.

—

A man and a woman want a woman and a man
or a man and a woman depending
on the man and the woman.

—

Once one gets what one wants once
one no longer wants it once

then one no longer wants it at all.

—

Yes then no. Yes and no? No.
Yes then no then yes and always
after yes comes no. Never always
yes, but always no. Always know
after yes comes no.

—

One wants what one wants
not what one wanted.

Were we twins earlier
we might have saved the other from learning to speak,

to speak dead, to speak dead romance, to speak dead romance
languages. Utter embouchure. The aftertaste of hurt knots the tongue,

an unripe persimmon. An echo tumbles from the mountain range
of a French horn, hunt long finished, rabbits interrupted

by bullets. Then skinned. Then opened wide. There is no translation
for rescue save breath. How we speak to and only to each other.

By the routine of lung. After years of half-formed, airtight Hebrew
the lonely heart's grammar relaxes, allows one vowel. U.

WHY I NEVER ADVANCED BEYOND THE FIRST LINE

And now you say you're sorry for saying
                    — failed first line

     1.

Then I'd say what my ex said
if it wasn't covered in carpet
sometime in the 90s.

     1.

I forgave her, you, her.

     1.

When did *you* become the right pronoun
for her? I have nothing to say to you.

     1.

And you me. And she me.

     1.

Nothing to say to her. I keep
braiding us into plaid.

     1.

I didn't cry the whole night through
and I didn't cry no river over you. Her.
Who are we kidding? You.

CONDITION

He had ribs *ding* How you doin? although he knew
I was vegan. *dong* Fine thank you and you? The pig,
I thought, such a pig. *ding* How you doin? *dong* Fine
thank you and you? And he belched low in the well
of his throat *ding* How you doin? as if I couldn't hear it.
dong Fine thank you and you? He belched the lowest
organ pedal in his throat *ding* How you doin? and did
not excuse himself or press his chest but *dong* Fine thank you
and you? kept chewing with the napkin balled up *ding*
How you doin? in his non-dominant hand to dab his *dong*
Fine thank you and you? flaming forehead. The pig, I thought. *ding*
How you doin? The waitress asked, *dong* Fine thank you
and you? Any dessert? And he made a show of calculating the tip,
selecting a credit card, placing it in the bill folder *ding* How you doin?

so I'd remember, as he held open my front door with his *dong*
Fine thank you and you? elbow, letting out the heat,
the cost of my hunger, the cost of his. *ding* How you doin?
When he dipped his rib mouth low to mine *dong* Fine
thank you and you? my belly was already descending
like an old pregnant dog. *ding* How you doin? He said,
Are you going to invite me in?

SEEKS SAME

You love me best
when you don't love me
openly.

SEEKS SOUL MATE

The answer
as I knew all along
is no one and ever.

III

Right. The fish. Right. The fish shakes its sequins
like an angry neck. Right. Small pond, backwater fish.
Right. Backward unicellular parents. Right. Who died
violently. Right. Aneurysms. Right. The fish grew
legs and walked right on shore. Right. It died
the first few times. Right. Natural causes. Right.
The time it didn't die it looked like a woman
climbing stairs to take teaspoons of cough syrup
to her child. Right. All the other times it looked
like a man. Right. Right. Right. Right. Its gills grew
into thalidomide arms. Right. It rolled around
like it was breading itself. Right. And said,
Ma, thinly, *Ma.* Right. Don't feel sorry for it. Right.
If a tree falls. Right. None of this happened
overnight, you understand. Right. It took millions
of years to grow a nose. Right. Then the rest
of the ocean emerged on ships. Right. Wearing hats.
Right. Hats. Right.

The hat. What? The hat was. What? The hat was being? What?
Worn. What? By an unseen head that spoke slowly in fifths.
What? C. G. C. What? It had a buckle and a waist. What?
It had a body and a waist. What? The hat was always taller
than a man. What? Men balanced steeples on their heads
then entire skylines. What? The hat disappeared into the sky.
What? Sometimes the hat was made of thorns. What? Sometimes
it was made of light and hovered two inches in the air. What?
But usually it was black and made of blacks on the outside
and canned fish on the inside. What? You heard right. What?
It eventually needed more fabric for its brim. What? Because
the sun was closer to the earth in those days. What? So the fish
swam west. What? Because of the sun, possibly, not the hat.
What? So. What? The hat tore itself in half when it turned south.
What? It smothered one of its most famous heads. What? That
was the end of that. What? It lost the buckle. What? Stuck
letters and logos and round gold stickers on itself. What?
All over. What? All over.

Try finding your mind last place
you left it — with your glasses or on the stunned passport photo
or staring at the anus of an airplane or at a hijabbed woman
as she re-packs her liquids, gels, aerosols — and doubtless
it's gone, mind, gone on without you like an ex-husband.

Better: try to map how it got from mugshot to
ex-husband in the twenty-five seconds you left it
unattended, how it tra-la-la-ed off with a stranger
and a waffle cone through the airport's neural pathways
and instead you will find only a grainy aerial photograph of it,
mind, facedown in a nearby river, floating in the sludge
of taped-up specs and aircraft fins and childhood orthodontics
and visitation rights and —

Then your attention returns to you
from the other side of the airport, in a babydoll dress, not so
much bored as bleached, dancing *one two cha cha cha*
and waving a dandelion like a semaphore. For me?
you say. For you.

                                    Against
the gym wall you practice backhands — not *you* but you
know what I mean — and the balls come back always. Again

you think swallowing eyeballs will not be like swallowing
beer caps or batteries — what I mean

                                    is the balls come back
and your stomach is neither a butterfly conservatory
nor a front-load washer — come back on a silver tray
with toothpicks in them: try me, sorry,

                                    again: Over lunch break
you cry forty years in the restroom then soap your face
with *fine thank you* and you

                                    go back to work, go back into the white
light of the copier that bends headlights into your eyes.
Fourteen, fifteen times the car slams into your head — sorry —
your head — sorry I can't help myself — your head then.

Fluffing their lopsided afro puffs in a public washroom
two black girls say some black girl look like a dude.

—

In a public mirror applying concealer with their pinkies
two black girls say some black girl talk like a valkyrie.

—

On a white tablecloth some black girl dreadlocks her fingers
waiting for two black girls to emerge threaded together.

—

Clopping from the washroom two maga girls in pumps
dragon-talk some black girl with hands to their mouths.

—

Two black girls want to hear some black girl spit ghetto
but she sucks on her fork and says the lamb is so-so.

                                                    which is tiny,
smaller than a baby's clubbed print on a birth certificate,
smaller than the mother's signature, more the size
of a bee's hoof, I walk to work twice a week, several miles,
knee-deep in exhaust.
                    The walk is the same as the walk
to primary school X

                    X only alone, and with strip mall awnings
instead of pomme cythere trees and at the diagonal a parking lot
instead of a field with goat droppings but no goats.

Our shoes were stuffed with cotton or newspaper. I was wearing
my brother's old hightops and hoping, in the hush-hush of my heart,
that I would outgrow him, that my mother would keep a cut-out
of my foot in her handbag and go to Bata
                                    when there interposed
a Jack Spaniard. Stung me on the eyelid. For being such a wicked,
wicked boy. This is what I think about when I think about
being mugged in the parking lot — a bigger foot, the Jack Spaniard's
buzz like a track laid over *Gimme your wallet.* He will wear
a bandana over his face. *I ain't playin with you, fool. Your watch too.*
And the ring. He will not want what I want
to leave behind. Nobody wants my trash, my old shoes,
my *wah wah* stories about back in the day, my foul rag and bone shop,
the baritone with beagle eyes who keeps the till, humming,
Nobody knows the trouble until *glory hallelujah.*

The phrase patience plays
to keep the heart pumped, the hands ready for a deluge
of quarters, goes something like *maybe, maybe*
or *this time, this time.*

You're at a grade 8 dance.
The streamers have already collapsed. Your hair too.
Firstname Lastname has not looked at you. Yet.
This song, this song, he will see me. Faith as random
as mirror ball light. *He will see me, he won't see me.*
Behind each ear, an eighth note of perfume.

Already patience has set you next to someone else,
two pill bottles in a medicine cabinet.

SATIE'S GNOSSIENNE NO. 3

        Be careful early. And watch out
for the light that warns, *Seul, pendant un instant.*
You are. Happily ever.

        A moment later you will be
tres perdu and will need to *ouvrez la tête,* whatever
that means.

        A stepmother will leave you
in the forest until your nails grow into clefs. What
trouble

        in the left hand,
the handful of dirt, the snowball of dirt, Satie
leaves for you.

        He's having you,
necktied and heeled: you've been asked to go
to a museum,

        an exhibit of female torsos
made from breadcrumbs, that sort of thing.
People go *mm* in their throats.

        If you take Satie seriously,
then you hear grief, just the far corner of it,
and separate from you:

        the snoring — or is it moaning —
woman in the hospital bed next to the friend
you came to see.

That anyone could save
the young from their soca and smoke, from the prow or body
of another young. They hold the alphabet
in the boat of their hands to drink. No. To throw
on their faces.

And it came to pass that a hooded one,
a boy filled with smoke, fell among gangbangers who wrote
graffiti on his face with a boxcutter and took all that he had,
even his smoke, and rolled away in bass.
O sacred head
now wounded that anyone by button bursting and rib depart
might save thee.

The hand from the Sistine Chapel
uncoils a paperclip and sticks it in the dimple marked *reset*.

A get-out-of-jail card, the actual card, along with property,
Boardwalk or Park Place, a railroad station.

The state issues each prisoner a smiling border collie,
which will die quietly and painfully sixteen years later
with its jaw flat along the floor.
                              The first year out
a hotel-sized life: white towels, tiny bottles of shampoo and bars
of soap, cable, a Bible and the Yellow Pages in a drawer.

Heaped plates of food from an aging mother, arthritic,
because her boy was lost and now is found. A father
who is tanning to leather in front of a TV on a recliner.

Each one gets an email address but no cell
phone. A job with the government, an adjustable chair,
a lunch break, a Big Gulp, a retro Harvey's
across the street,
                    only after he writes every five-paragraph essay
he missed and reports on the bacteria culture in his petri dish,
and factors hundreds of polynomials and can conjugate
aller into the *passé composé*.

                    Every other Thursday, pay day,
he goes to the barbershop, which comes standard in the fantasy
with at least one ignant brotha, and gets his hair cut for what will be
a series of bad dates, Saturday nights with divorced women,
before finding, finally, a no-nonsense woman, one who needs
to be picked up from work. *5:15. Be there.* A kiss behind
the wipers when she gets in the truck. (A truck.)
                                        A wife who thinks
what the master really needs is a medallion. *If you say so.*
It'll frame the light like a halo. *I guess.* That conversation,
as they approach the Niagara border and he presents the passports
of all four in the car — wife, boy thumbing a handheld videogame,
little girl in a car seat. To have the passports returned. To be
wished well by a man in uniform and called *sir.*

HANGMAN

Is there an *n?*
There is only *n.*

—

The chin slips
backward. Immediately
the mind shrinkwraps
"- - -   - -   - - -   - - - - -   - - -   - - -, n - - - - -?"

—

Is there an *r?* Two.
Is there a *u?* Two.

A *c?* There goes your head.
A *b?* And now your neck
in the noose.

—

Why lynch
a stick man

for what
I can't say

and what
you can't guess?

—

I make it difficult, true,
but possible, clearing only
what you need to get in:
two tire paths in the heart's
snowy driveway.

EXCEPT THAT IT FEELS LIKE A POCKET OF FAT AROUND THE HEART

like the limp wrists of the three women behind Bob Marley,

like a room full of them in the wallpaper, a chatroom
of profile photos, four across five down,

                                   like a certain slant of light
through the west windows, the frayed tongue of an open hymnal,

like the Listerine or Polident heat of an old man's mouth, a drawer
of unaired Christmas sweaters, like *please,* yes, like *please.*

Seeing his skin, stretched transparent
like plastic over a Styrofoam meat tray,
and the striation of his muscles, an illustration
from an anatomy textbook,
                              Job's wife suggests
he root around a high-end dumpster, then gives him
details as if she has done it before, exactly
which streets and at what time and what to say
should he get caught. He has rights.
                              I see his soul
step out of his body. It is white and transparent
and wears the same clothes. Rights, she's right.
She is all so edible.

EXCEPT THAT DESPAIR FEELS, REMASTERED

like a dance mix, a dance, a dance mix, a dance
done a decade too late

                       except that it feels, that it feels, that it feels
like techno in the head, insufferable rubble, like ping pong
on Atari, the 80s, *please*

                  o

                   please, like a voice re-touched
by a yawn about to overtake you, the mouth
keeps opening and opening

                    it feels like, it feels like it feels
like a muppet the inside of a muppet's mouth is felt

Many options, many options. Copy. Multifunctional,
you could say. Copy. You could say, I've been fun. Copy.
Off and on. Copy. I can staple a bow in my hair. Copy. I'd prefer
not to. Copy. But I'm not particular. Copy. I read everything
you give me. Copy. Closely. Copy. I know, for instance,
that the footer of the email from the immigration attorney
was appended by a Blackberry Wireless Device. Copy.
I read everything you give me. Copy. Money. Copy.
What I don't like I eat or spit up. Copy. I am not acting
like a child. You're a child. Copy. Once the toner
cartridge exploded in the room behind the secretaries.
Copy. And a licensed technician came in and talked
to me for an hour. Copy. *How did that make you feel?*
and so on. Copy. I will jam occasionally, arbitrarily
bite your hand. Copy. Gemini. Copy. Two-sided. Copy.
Old man with wrinkled dugs. Copy. Who knows what.
Copy. I read everything. Copy. I read everything. Copy.
Copy. Copy.

My ears open before my eyes after a night of not enough
sleep, not enough night. They run over with birdsong. You die
in reverse apparently: the eyes close, then the ears. Which is why
people say keep speaking, say everything you can, to the dying,
stop talking to the dead.

                                  The birds open their mouths
before their eyes. I thought that I heard them speaking
to me, to the dying. I thought that I heard them sing
to each other. They sing — don't they sing? — they cry
better in the dark, eyes closed against it. So much depends
on their prayers.

Against the dark, one bird cries: *Listen to me.* Another cries:
To me. Another: *Do Lord.* Another: *Do Lord.* Another: *Do*
remember me. Another: *Me.* Another: *Love me.* Another:
Or leave me. Another: *But don't leave me.* Another: *Lonely.*
Another: *No.* Another: *No.* Another: *Oh no.* Another: *No.*

— there was cause for alarm — I can help — at thirty —
the next person — thirty-five — in line — and forty —
over here — I ran out of my body — I can help —
and watched fire trucks — the next person — scream and spit —
in line — over my faulty wiring — over this way —
and when finally boarded up — I can help — condemned —
the next person — spray-painted in the night by teenagers
in sagging jeans — standing in line — I thought maybe
that we could actually like totally you know — this way —
basically — I can help — there was nothing I could say —
the next person — there was nothing — in line — I could say —
over here — there was cause for alarm — I can help — the building
dreams of the marks of children ascending up the doorframe
year after year — the next person in line — Dylan age three
and four and five — over here — but — no one and ever — I can help —
copy — the next person — no one and ever — I can help —
what? — over here — I can — no one and ever — help — right —
I can — no one and ever — help

There is a word for people who rub against others on crowded buses.

What if you stuck your earbuds up your nose instead?

I am tired of *understanding* transitive but I am tired of nonsense as well.

It seems sometimes like you talk to everyone but me.

I had a girlfriend who once explained that to me and only now
    do I understand.

The word is *frotteur.* Sounds French but there is a lot of Japanese porn
    I haven't seen of businessmen and school girls engaged in *frotteurism.*

You don't care and you don't care to pretend you find me —

I don't care but I guess I have always wanted to be in a British costume
    drama where people wear feathered eye masks and dance palm to palm.

Although — will you forgive me? — I prefer you when you eat your yogurt
    in the corner of my eye and sob little up bows of vibrato.

Once a box toppled and scraped my shins, skinned me, pretty much, alive.

Indeed you are getting crispier the longer you keep those things
    plugged into your ears.

Aren't you tired of understanding things?

I listened and all the music after the 1880s is terrible. I mean, just awful.

Don't give me that look. Give me that one. Don't give me that finger.

Aren't you tired of being understanding?

And of course there was no music before Bach or art before the cave
    paintings at Lascaux. Or animals for that matter.

I gave you my seat and all you can say is *thank you* and stare blankly
    at my crotch.

I'm occasionally tempted to steal luggage from the baggage belt and
    rummage through your underwear.

I got wireless shoelaces the other day. What's the rest of the joke?

Pity that you got a smart phone and lost the lost look you used to wear.

Would you condescend a little lower please?

I preferred you.

I might be wrong. There's a chance you may have been right all along.

TOO FAR

One day you will go too far.
Run out of breadcrumbs. Stub your toe
against the pot of gold. Singe your horse's face
on the sunset.

Igniting into red, like a sumac,
you will blast the wrong person with the wrong words
— perhaps *capitalist patriarch* or *hegemonic bureaucrat* —
and make smoke of your job. Security will watch you pack
your belongings into a Xerox box in case, as a final protest,
you try to steal the company stapler.

You will go too far
into that first night. Oh gentle, do not go past the caution signs:
the yellow diamond, the fever, *hello.* You will want to but do not,
not even with your eyes, undress the wrong brown sugar,
kiss the wrong neck, roll underwear down your unshaved thighs.

The distance bends into blue. Behind the *sfumato,*
the horizon gives way to canvas. God overdrawn.
He holds up a dented hand. *High five.* No. *Goodbye.* Close.
Stop.

Because if you keep going you will go too far. You will reach
the last page, the white hell below, and have to burn it over or turn from — it
will come, your time will, all good things come.

ACKNOWLEDGEMENTS

I am grateful to Palazzo Rinaldi in Italy for a residency that enabled the completion of this manuscript. Special thanks also to the Cave Canem Foundation and Vermont Studio Center. I have been extremely fortunate to work with Freehand Books under the intelligence, creativity, integrity, and warmth of Robyn Read, Sarah Ivany, Natalie Olsen, and, for this collection, Owen Percy.

The epigraph to the collection is taken from Claudia Rankine's *Don't Let Me Be Lonely* (Graywolf, 2004).

Some of these poems were a finalist for the CBC Literary Prize. "Rings" was a finalist for the *Malahat* Long Poem Prize. "Please Print Clearly in Block Capital Letters" won third place in *Arc Poetry Magazine* 2011 Poem of the Year Competition.

Thanks to the editors of the following publications in which these poems first appeared:

Arc: "Please Print Clearly in Block Capital Letters"; *The Caribbean Writer:* "To reduce the size of my carbon footprint"; *Confrontation:* "Ten couplets for parking lots at night"; *The Dos Passos Review:* "Office Suite"; *Ellipsis:* "Idioglossia"; *Fiddlehead:* "Five words I've wanted to see in Pope," "He will tell me later the story of the woman he has been alluding to all day," and "Missed connections: Walmart automotive dept — w4m — (Lunenburg MA)"; *Folio:* "Hay" and "Nutrition Facts"; *Mythium:* "Too Far"; *Rattle:* "Hero"; *Ruminate:* "Comfort"; *Straylight:* "Out of work"; *The Windsor Review:* "American History I," "The romance novel," "Satie's Gnossienne No. 3," "Bore," and "Prisoner Fantasy"; *The Worcester Review:* "Schumann's Arabesque, Op. 18," which was also awarded Honourable Mention for the Frank O'Hara Prize.